My goal is to

Entertain ■ **Educate** ■ **Empower**

children by telling meaningful Stories
while teaching Sign Language!

Mr.C

The Haunted Baseball Park
Being Brave & Smart Story
ASL - American Sign Language Book for Kids and Beginners
Stories and Signs with Mr.C - Book 8

Story Written by Mr.C - Randall Clarkson
Design & Illustrations by Deonna Clarkson

© 2016 by RDCmedia—Randall & Deonna Clarkson

All rights reserved. No part of this book may be used or reproduced in any way without the written and signed permission of the author, except in the case of brief quotations embodied in critical articles or reviews.

StoriesAndSigns.com

Positive Repetition

is a learning method that rewards your child in a positive way.

- **Read through the story in one sitting**. Note that the words printed in color correspond with the characters in the pictures above.

- **Go back to the beginning of the book and begin to sign**. Your child will see the signs as an actual part of the story which is now familiar to them.

- **Parents can sign the two signs** shown on each page and have your child copy you. Try not to touch their hands as they first struggle to find the sign themselves. They are exploring how they can manipulate on their own.

- **Note the underlined words**. These are the sign language words which were read and signed earlier in the story.

- **Continue to re-read each book** until all the signs listed in the back are learned. Your child will love re-reading the books and the feeling of mastering the signs more and more.

- **Use these new sign language words** throughout the day, reinforcing them to memory.

The **Positive Repetition** of the sign language words will

engage the memory, entertain the heart & **empower your child.**

Thank you for giving your child the gift of Sign Language!

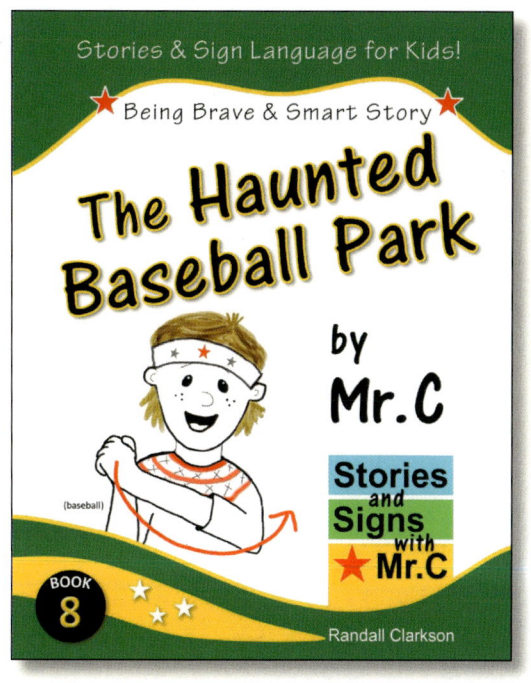

The Haunted Baseball Park

BOOK 8 of the **Stories and Signs** Series

by

Mr.C

Randall Clarkson

"At the end of this book,
I have two special gifts just for you!
Be sure and use your hands to
learn the sign words!"

Mr.C

Do you know what it means to be brave?

It means...

"I don't say I can't, I say I will try!"

This is the story about a brave girl named Dani who taught a lesson to her whole city. She was brave when she solved a scary baseball mystery that no one else could figure out.

Did you know that in every city in the United States there is a baseball park?

It might be a small field at a school or a big baseball park for professional teams.

Do *you* have a baseball park in *your* city? Have *you* ever gone to a game?

At every baseball game there are four groups of people…can *you* guess who they are?

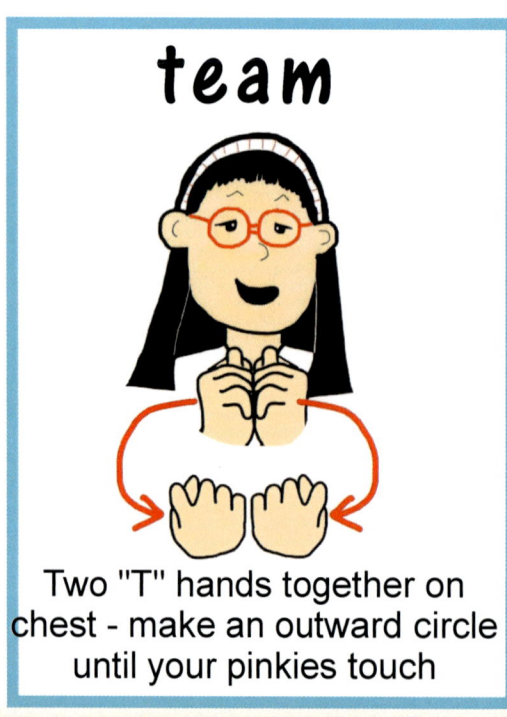

1. The Home Team

The home team is the team that is playing in their own baseball park.

Each of the teams takes turns either hitting the ball and running bases or catching the ball out in the field.

Have *you* ever played baseball?

Do *you* like hitting or catching the ball best?

2. The Visiting Team

The visiting team comes to the home team's baseball park for the game.

They sit on benches in the dugout while they wait for their turn to hit the ball. If they swing and miss, it is called a strike.

Three strikes and they are called out. Three outs and it's the other team's turn to try to hit the ball.

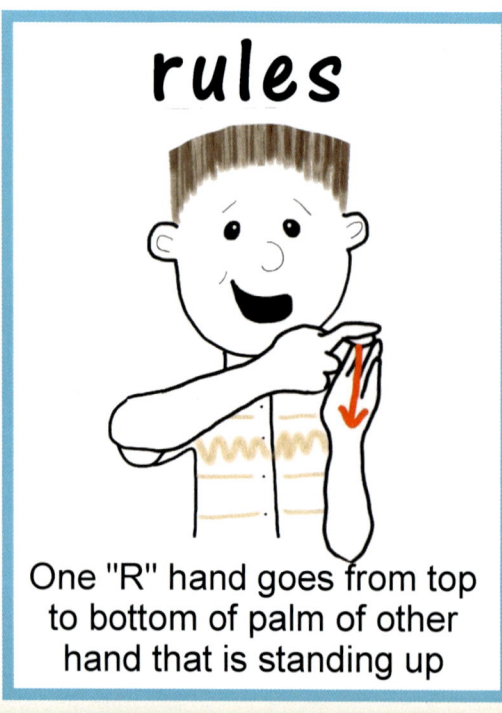

3. The Umpire & Team Manager

The umpire makes sure everyone plays by the rules in the baseball game.

Each team has a leader…that's their Team Manager. They teach the players how to play baseball and what the rules of the game are.

It's important that everyone plays by the rules and has fun playing the game.

hotdog

One hand cupped like a bun - other hand has two fingers straight like the hotdog - put hotdog inside bun hand

soda pop

Poke pointer finger and thumb inside fist of other hand - pull upward then down to slap the top of your fisted hand

4. The Baseball Fans

The last group at the baseball game is the crowd of people that comes to watch the game.

Baseball fans like to loudly cheer for their team. They eat hotdogs, peanuts, popcorn, and candy. They drink from juice boxes and soda pop or water bottles.

Most of all…they like to yell for their team!

Once there was a baseball game in a city not too far from here. The two teams came to play baseball and the crowd of people came to watch, eat, drink and cheer loudly for their team.

Those people that came to watch and eat did something *very* wrong.

They threw their litter and drink bottles on the ground under their benches!

Is that the right thing to do with their garbage?

No!

That is called littering.

As the game went on, it became darker and the wind began to blow.

The pitcher was in the middle of the grass field and was just about to throw the ball when...

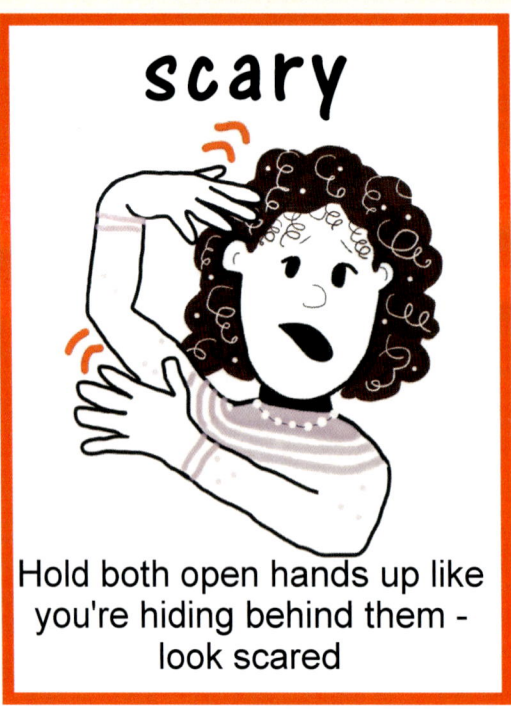

...there was a scary sound.

Not just a little sound—but a big, loud, scary sound!

"What was that?," the pitcher asked the other baseball players. They didn't know.

Everyone became quiet and listened...

WHOOO!

WHOOO!

WHOOO!

...came the sound again.

Someone yelled, "It's a GHOST!!!" and everyone ran away from the baseball park before the end of the game.

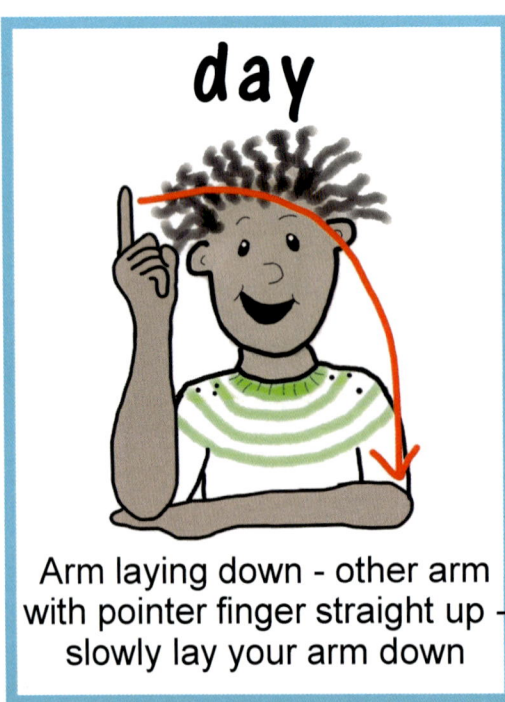

After the scary sound, nobody would come back to watch any games and no teams would come back to play any games.

Everyone said that it was haunted by the Baseball Ghost.

They wouldn't even walk by the ball park during the day.

Do *you* think there was a Baseball Ghost making that noise?

The Mayor of the city got on TV and said that it was so sad that they couldn't play baseball and watch the games at the park anymore.

"I have an idea!" the Mayor told the news reporters.

"Is anyone brave enough to spend the night in the park and get rid of the Baseball Ghost?"

Would *you* do it?

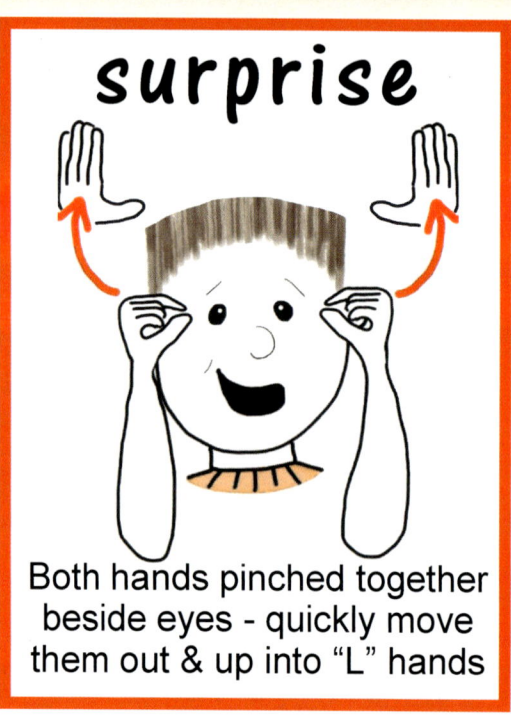

"I have a special surprise for anyone that is brave enough to do this!" the Mayor exclaimed, "Anyone?"

It was quiet for a long time.

"Yes...I'll do it tonight!" Dani called out, "because I don't say I can't, I say I will try!"

Dani's Dad gave his brave girl a big hug.

Would *you* be as brave as Dani?

Dani's Mom packed her a sandwich, an apple and juice to take with her that night.

Dani's Dad packed his things so that he could go with her to the baseball park.

What do *you* think they should take with them?

Sleeping bags?

Flashlights?

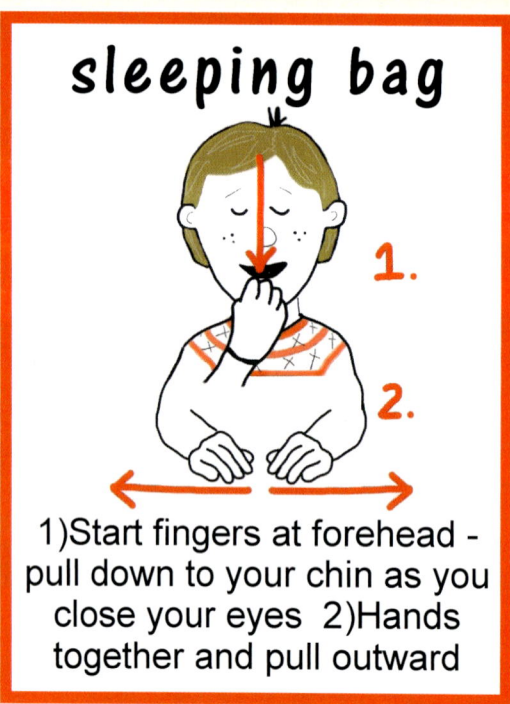
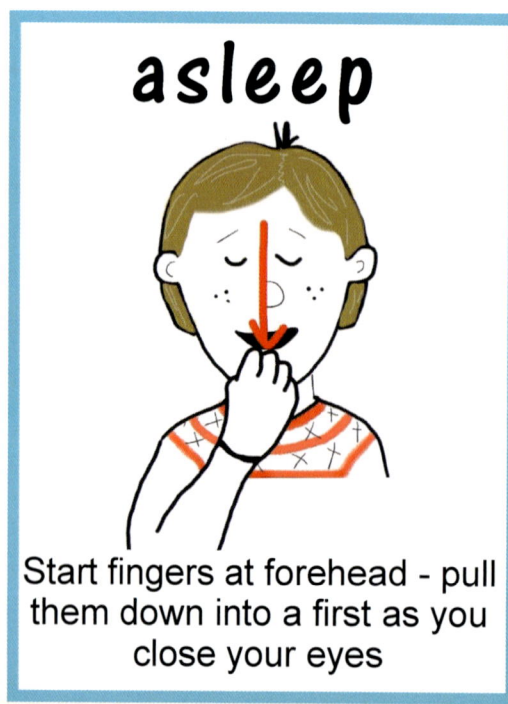

That night Dani and her Dad unrolled their sleeping bags out on the pitcher's mound and crawled inside. She waited for it to get dark…and she fell asleep.

Later that night the wind began blowing and Dani woke up to that scary sound…

WHOOO! WHOOO! WHOOO!

Dani jumped out of her sleeping bag and turned on her flashlight. She shined it all around but she didn't see a ghost.

The sound seemed to be louder near the benches. Dani walked closer and closer to the sound.

When she slowly turned the corner at the end of the benches, she stopped.

"AH-HA!" exclaimed Dani as she shined her flashlight. Then she started to laugh and she laughed some more!

She laughed all the way back to her sleeping bag. She climbed back in and went to sleep.

In the morning the Mayor came to the ball park.

blow

Purse lips - make "O" sign by your mouth - move hand outward & open up fingers

no

Pointer and tall fingers on top - thumb on the bottom - snap them together

"The Baseball Ghost is really the sound that the wind makes when it blows across the empty bottles," Dani explained.

"Are you saying there is no ghost?" asked the Mayor as they all started to laugh.

"No Baseball Ghost, just smelly garbage!" said Dani as she joined the laughter.

Have you ever tried blowing across a soda pop bottle, making a scary sound?

brave

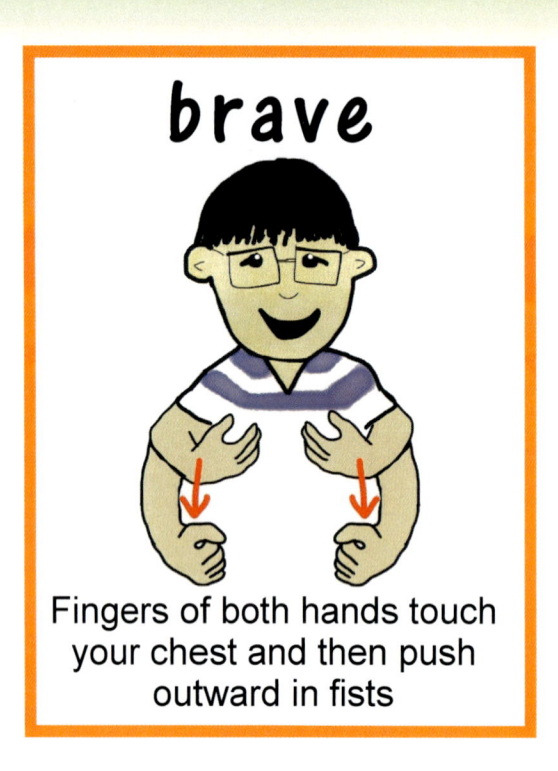

Fingers of both hands touch your chest and then push outward in fists

ice cream

Pretend like you're holding an ice cream cone with your right hand and licking it

The Mayor said that from now on this day will be...

"Be brave like Dani Day!"

"Let's all have an ice cream party!"

No more garbage!

No more ghost sounds!

Lots of baseball games!

Download your free CERTIFICATE just for reading this book!

- Place to write your name
- List of Sign Words to practice
- Show your family & friends!

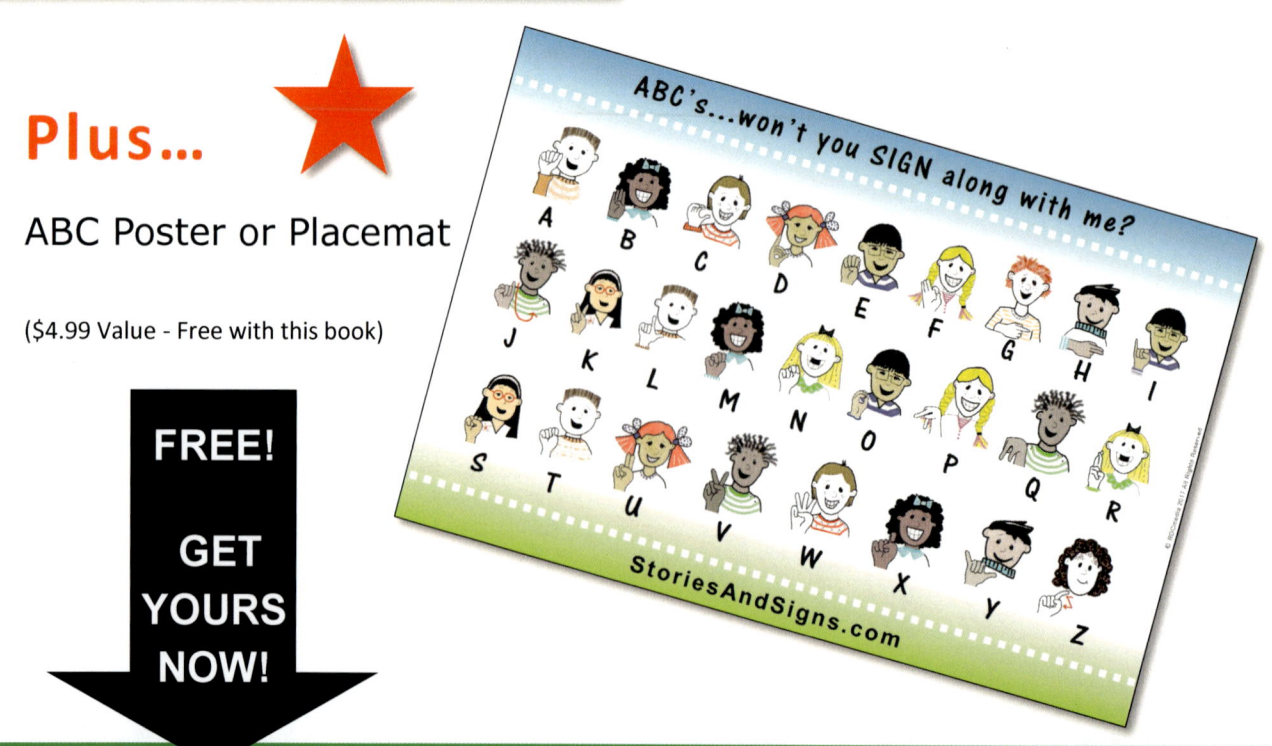

Plus...

ABC Poster or Placemat

($4.99 Value - Free with this book)

FREE! GET YOURS NOW!

StoriesAndSigns.com/Gifts

More **Stories and Signs** with Mr.C

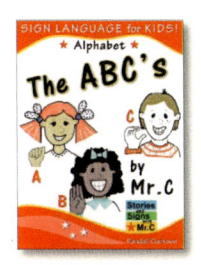

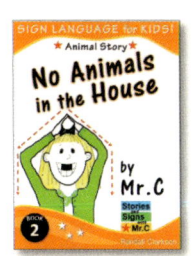

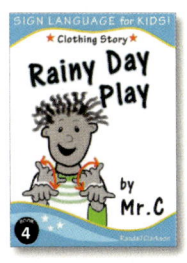

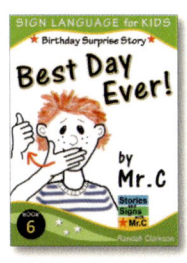

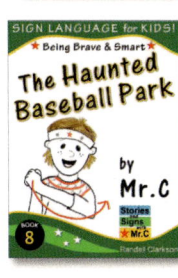

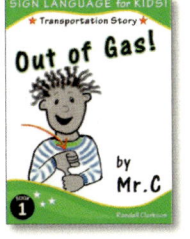

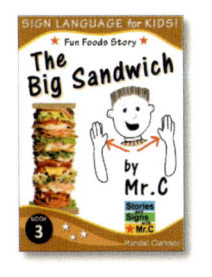

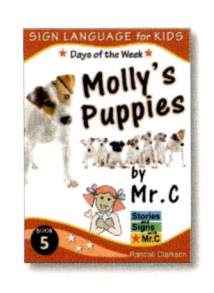

★ **The ABC's** — ASL Alphabet Signs

#1 **Out of Gas!** — Transportation Story

#2 **No Animals in the House** — Animals Story

#3 **The Big Sandwich** — Fun Foods Story

#4 **Rainy Day Play** — Indoor & Outdoor Play & Colors

#5 **Molly's Puppies** — Days of the Week

#6 **Best Day Ever!** — Birthday Surprise

#7 **Company is Coming!** — Cleaning My Room

#8 **Haunted Baseball Park** — Being Brave & Smart

Available at **StoriesAndSigns.com** or **Amazon.com/Author/RandallClarkson**

Can you Sign these words from the Story?

- brave
- girl
- baseball
- park
- home
- team
- game
- ball
- play
- rules
- hotdog
- soda pop
- watch
- eat
- littering
- wind
- scary
- big
- quiet
- ghost
- walk
- day
- sad
- idea
- surprise
- hug
- Mom
- Dad
- sleeping bag
- asleep
- jump
- flashlight
- stop
- laugh
- blow
- no
- ice cream

(ice cream)

The more I practice, the better I become! - Mr.C

We would like to dedicate this book to
our five amazing Grandchildren...

Meadow ♥ Logan ♥ Dani ♥ Austin ♥ Drew

...and the thousands of kids who
have learned sign language words
while laughing & enjoying our stories.

Mr.C AUTHOR/TEACHER/PAPA
Mrs.C ILLUSTRATOR/GRAMA

Made in the USA
Columbia, SC
19 November 2020